Before reading this book ... to know:

· two or more letters ca

· the spelling <ear> can re ... ear', 'air' as in 'bear', 'ar' as in 'heart' an

This book introduces:

· the spelling <ear> for the sounds 'ear', 'air', 'ar' and 'er'

· text at 2 syllable level

High-frequency words:

was, dark, put, gone, what

Vocabulary:

gripped with fear - was very frightened

appeared - could be seen

Talk about the story

Bear is afraid of the dark. When Viv switches off the light, he is gripped with fear. He sees a monster on the wall. Will it get him?

Reading Practice

Alternative pronunciations for the spelling <ear>.
Practise blending these sounds into words:

'air'	'er'	'ar'	'ear'
bear	earn	heart	near
pear	heard	hearth	fear
tear	learn		dear
wear	pearl		hear
swear	earth		spear
	search		clear
	early		appear

Bear's Fears

Ted, the bear, was afraid of the dark. When Viv switched off the light, Ted was gripped with fear.

Ted stared into the night. What was that banging he could hear? He heard his heart thumping.

Ted put his hands over his ears.

A monster appeared on the wall.

Ted feared it would get him.

Tears dropped onto his soft fur.

"Oh dear! The monster will tear me apart!" he heard himself say.

Ted, the bear, crept under the blanket to be near to Viv. His heart stopped thumping.

The next day, Ted saw the pear tree and the hat stand. The monster had gone and so had Ted's fears.

Questions for discussion:

- Why was Ted gripped with fear?

- Why did Ted cover his ears?

- What did Ted find out the next morning?

Game with <ear> words

Play as pelmanism or use for reading practice. Enlarge and photocopy the page twice on two different colours of card. Cut the cards up to play.
Ensure the players sound out the words.

bear	ear	learn
heart	wear	clear
dear	pear	earth
appear	hearth	swear